GiRL TALK

How to Deal with Friendship Conflicts

For my best friend
— R.W.

For all the young women in the Oakdale Ward,
what great friends to have!
— T.M.

ISBN 0-439-86644-8
Text copyright © 2006 Scholastic Inc.
Illustrations copyright © 2006 Scholastic Inc.
All rights reserved. Published by Scholastic Inc.
SCHOLASTIC and associated logos are trademarks and/or registered trademarks
of Scholastic Inc.

12 11 10 9 8 7 6 5 4 3 2   6 7 8 9 10 11/0

Printed in the U.S.A.
First printing, October 2006
Book design by Carla Siegel

GiRL TALK

How to Deal with Friendship Conflicts

by Robin Wasserman
Illustrated by Taia Morley

Scholastic Inc.
New York Toronto London Auckland Sydney
Mexico City New Delhi Hong Kong Buenos Aires

Rachel

Name: Rachel

Nickname: Red

Style: Artsy

Hobbies: Crafts, music, acting

Favorite Place: Theater (onstage!)

Favorite Sport: Swimming

Favorite Snack: Granola and yogurt

Hidden Talent: Always optimistic

Sometimes Known As: Drama Queen

Sam

Name: Samantha

Nickname: Sam

Style: Casual

Hobbies: Hiking, biking

Favorite Place: The gym

Favorite Sport: Soccer, skiing, sailing

Favorite Snack: Energy bar

Hidden Talent: Making people laugh

Sometimes Known As: The Athlete

JESSIE

Name: Jessica

Nickname: Jessie

Style: Girly

Hobbies: Reading, writing, babysitting

Favorite Place: The library

Favorite Sport: Tennis

Favorite Snack: Corn chips

Hidden Talent: Great Listener

Sometimes Known As: The Great Brain

Name: Elizabeth

Nickname: Libby

Style: Glam

Hobbies: Volunteering, cooking

Favorite Place: Anywhere with lots of people

Favorite Sport: Dance

Favorite Snack: Fruit salad

Hidden Talent: Never at a loss for words

Sometimes Known As: Party Girl

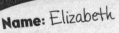

Libby

That's where we come in! Because we've been friends forever, we've seen it all. So we can help you deal with the worst of times—and help you celebrate the best of times. We all know life can be tough sometimes. And let's face it: Friendship's not always easy. But it's *always* worth it.

YOU WANNA FIGHT?

Even the best of friends fight.
Here are some of our greatest hits:

"This sweater is sooo cute. Jessie will never notice if I borrow it."

"MY FAVORITE SWEATER? I'LL NEVER FORGIVE YOU!"

"I am so BORED.
Let's play soccer."
"Uh, no thanks.
Let's paint our nails."
"Manicures?
BOR-ING!"
"Soccer?
PUH-LEASE!"
"Fine."
"Fine."
This stinks!

FIRST THINGS FIRST, LET'S FIGURE OUT YOUR FIGHTING STYLE. ANSWER THESE TRUE OR FALSE QUESTIONS AND FIND OUT WHAT YOU DO WHEN YOU'RE ONE HUNDRED PERCENT SURE THAT YOUR BFFS ARE WRONG, WRONG, WRONG.

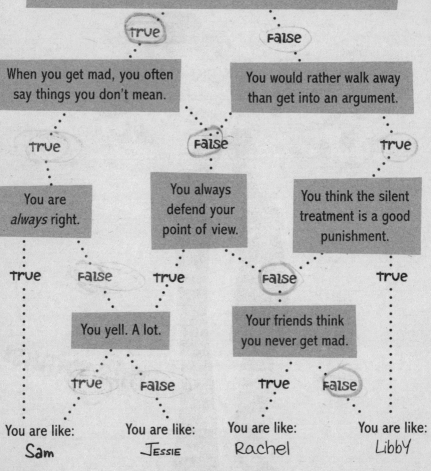

When you disagree with a friend, your friend always knows it.

true — When you get mad, you often say things you don't mean.

False — You would rather walk away than get into an argument.

true — You are *always* right.

False — You always defend your point of view.

true — You think the silent treatment is a good punishment.

true — You yell. A lot.

False — Your friends think you never get mad.

You are like: **Sam**

You are like: **Jessie**

You are like: **Rachel**

You are like: **Libby**

If you are like SAM:

Sam is a total hothead. And she thinks she's always right, no matter what anyone else says. She yells and yells until we get so tired we just give in. But Sam knows we hate it when she gets that way, so now she's trying to stay calmer and not be such a bully.

IF YOU ARE LIKE JESSIE:

Jessie never raises her voice, but she also never backs down when she thinks she's right. She always has a calm, rational argument to explain why she's thinking what she's thinking. She fights with her head, not her heart.

If you are like RACHEL:

Rachel is quiet and kind of shy, and she hates fighting more than anything in the world. So when she disagrees with us, she usually just keeps her mouth shut. We never even know anything is wrong. That means fewer fights for us—but it also means Rachel never gets what she wants. And she keeps everything inside, which isn't always healthy.

If you are like LIBBY:

Libby also hates fights—but that doesn't mean she doesn't get mad. When something doesn't go her way, she shuts her mouth and keeps it shut. It's called the silent treatment, and it drives us crazy. You can't argue with someone who's not arguing back. On the other hand, if Libby stays quiet, she can't explain why she thinks we're wrong. So she never convinces us she's right, either.

The best part about fighting is making up! These fights might sound kind of silly now, but trust us, at the time, they were huge! Here's how we got past the big blow-ups:

I'M NOT REALLY A BIG CLOTHES PERSON, BUT MY MOM BOUGHT ME A SWEATER FOR MY BIRTHDAY THAT I LOVED. LOVED— THAT'S PAST TENSE, BECAUSE A COUPLE WEEKS AFTER MY BIRTHDAY, LIBBY GOT HER HANDS ON IT. GOOD-BYE, SWEATER! IT'S NOT LIKE SHE EVEN ASKED ME TO BORROW IT. SHE JUST TOOK IT, AND THEN SHE RUINED IT. WAS I MAD? DOES A HYDROGEN ATOM ONLY HAVE ONE ELECTRON? THAT'S A DEFINITE YES. SO WHAT DID WE DO? LIBBY APOLOGIZED— A LOT. SHE DIDN'T THINK I CARED ABOUT CLOTHES AT ALL—BUT NOW SHE KNOWS TO ASK BEFORE SHE BORROWS ANY OF MY STUFF. AS FOR ME, I REALIZED THAT'S ALL IT WAS: STUFF. AND NO STUFF WILL EVER BE AS IMPORTANT TO ME AS LIBBY.

Rachel can be a little . . . forgetful. We're talking head-in-the-sky, always-asking-why, far-out spacey. I love her for it, but sometimes . . . ooh, it just makes me mad. Like when she says she'll meet me somewhere and then, poof! She forgets five seconds later. And there I am sitting all by myself, like a big fat loser. That's why we made a deal. Now when we make plans, Rachel writes them down—and because I know she's forgetful, I always call to remind her. And here's the best part: If she ever does forget me again, she has to buy me an ice-cream sundae. Now, that's what I call a happy ending!

So, Sam always wants to play soccer. Or football. Or run laps around the house. She never wants to try on makeup, or paint her nails, or help me bake cookies for the next meeting of my Endangered Earth club. We used to get into big fights about it all the time— and that was no fun at all, for either one of us. So we came up with a plan. A third of the time, we do what I want. A third of the time, we do what Sam wants. The rest of the time, we come up with something that we both like to do. And you know what? Sometimes it's kind of cool to try new stuff. Last week we played basketball. I broke a nail . . . but I also scored fourteen points!

Since You Asked ... ★ ★

Dear Friends 4-Ever,

I don't know what to do! Last week I beat my BFF at Scrabble. She never, ever loses, so I was superexcited. Except, guess what, she says I cheated! I told her there's no way I would do that. But she doesn't believe me! Now she's not speaking to me at all, and I'm even madder at her. I can't believe she doesn't trust me. I don't want to lose my BFF, but I also don't want to apologize for something I didn't do! Can you help?

Yours truly,
This Spells Trouble

Dear This Spells Trouble,

She may be a very good friend, but she doesn't sound like a very good loser, does she? I know you're mad, but no game should mean more than your friendship. You don't have to say you're sorry for something you didn't do—but you should still talk to your BFF. Just be honest: Tell her how she hurt your feelings, and why. But don't yell, and don't get mad. Just promise that you would never cheat, and ask her to trust you. You can even offer her a rematch. As long as you make up with each other, you're both winners!

Good luck!

Samantha   Rachel   Jessie   Libby

Quiz Time: Bring It On!

Are you passive or aggressive? Are you a stubborn steamroller or do you let people walk all over you? Take this quiz to find out!

bannah

1 It's Saturday afternoon and you're hanging out with your best buds. They want to go shopping. You want to go bike riding. You . . .

    a) Refuse to do anything until you get your way.

    b) Agree to go shopping, but only if they agree to go biking the next day.

    c) Go with them to the mall and pretend you think it's a great idea.

2 In the cafeteria, someone bumps into you, spilling fruit juice down the front of your favorite sweater. Then they start to walk away without even apologizing. You . . .

a) Chase after them and dump your soda over their head. Serves them right, after all.

b) Say, "Excuse me, but you just bumped into me and ruined my sweater."

c) Keep quiet and dry yourself off. Why make a fuss?

3 Your mom baked a batch of cookies for you and your BFF. Now there's only one left, and your friend wants it. But you do, too. You . . .

a) Eat the cookie. After all, your house, your mom, your dessert . . . right?

b) Suggest you break the cookie in half, or flip a coin for it.

c) Tell her she can have it. It's just a cookie.

4 You can't find your lunch money, and you think the boy who sits behind you might have taken it. You . . .

a) Accuse him, and if he denies it, start going through all of his stuff and telling everyone that he stole your money.

b) Ask him if he knows what happened to your lunch money, and if he says no, quietly talk to your teacher about what might have happened.

c) Skip lunch that day and eat a big dinner.

5 This girl at school is spreading rumors about you. This week, she's telling everyone that you smell. You . . .

a) Tell everyone that she still wets the bed.

b) Pretend it doesn't upset you, but tell her to stop spreading rumors. Make sure your friends let everyone know that you do *not* smell.

c) Wonder if you should start taking more showers.

**Now count up the number of
As, Bs, and Cs you answered.**

Mostly As: Control Freak

You know what you want, and you're going to get it, no matter what. Everyone else better get out of the way. But remember that you're not the only person in the world, and you're not the only one with feelings. And sometimes the best way to make yourself happy is by making sure everyone else is happy, too.

Mostly Bs: You Win Some, You Lose Some

You stand up for yourself and what you believe in, but you try not to hurt anyone else in the process. You're all about compromise, finding a solution that works for everyone. Your attitude depends on the situation. Sometimes you're loud and demanding; sometimes you're quiet and laid-back. But you're always flexible, and you always get results.

Mostly Cs: The Human Doormat

You would rather be miserable than make a fuss. You don't tell anyone what you want because you're scared you won't get it. So instead, you just deal with whatever comes along. You let people take advantage of you because you're afraid to tell them no. There's nothing wrong with wanting other people to be happy, but what you want matters, too. So don't be afraid to go for it!

Fighting Fair

Is there such a thing as a good fight? You bet. In a bad fight, everyone walks away with angry faces and hurt feelings. But in a good fight—a fair fight—everyone gets to talk about their problems and figure out a way to solve them. Since that's the only kind of fight *we* ever want to have with one another, we all signed this *friendship contract.* It means that when we do fight, we promise to follow the rules. And that's a lot easier to do when you come up with the rules *before* the fight. Now you and your friends can make up your own set of rules—and make sure that every fight you have is a good fight!

FAIR FIGHT CONTRACT

In order to preserve our friendship and form a more perfect union, we, the undersigned, agree that in any and all cases of friendly disagreement, we will follow the rules as described below:

1) No physical violence. Ever. Under any circumstances. That means no wrestling, kicking, punching, biting, or hair pulling (and that means you, too, Sam!).

2) No personal insults. We will fight about what people *do*, not about what people *are*. No saying that someone "always" does this or "never" does that. We will disagree about specific events or actions, but we'll always remember that in the end, we're BFF. And that's forever.

3) No bringing up stuff that happened in the past that doesn't have anything to do with our fight.

4) No yelling.

   a) If you do feel like you need to yell, stop talking. Take deep breaths. Count to one hundred. If that doesn't work, leave the room for five minutes.

5) No interrupting. (And that goes for you, too, Libby—yes, even when you have something superimportant to say that you think really, really, really can't wait. It can.)

6) Come up with at least three ideas for how you can solve your problem and end the fight. Don't stop until you find a solution that both of you agree on.

7) Never go to bed angry.

   a) If you fight and fight and fight and fight and can't find a compromise, don't walk away mad. Don't stop speaking to each other. Instead, take a break from the fight. Remind yourselves why you are friends. Each person must come up with two things she likes about the other person, and two happy memories of their friendship.

We agree to uphold all of the above rules in the course of any fight. If we fail to do so, and have an unfair fight with a friend, the penalty will be the following:

A) We will apologize to that friend.

B) The next time we disagree with that friend, we will give in immediately and do whatever she wants.

C) We will owe that friend one extra-large ice-cream sundae with hot fudge sauce, whipped cream, chopped nuts, caramel, and a big red cherry on top. Yum.

Samantha   Rachel   Jessie   Libby

Now you can come up with your own
Fair Fight Contract **on a separate sheet of paper.**

The Art of Compromise

ACCORDING TO WEBSTER'S DICTIONARY, A COMPROMISE IS "THE EMBODIMENT OF CONCESSION OR ADJUSTMENT."

According to my definition, a compromise means "You give a little, I give a little, and we both end up with at least a little of what we want. Which means we both end up happy."

Imagine there's a long red stripe painted across the floor, and when you and your BFF fight, you're on opposite sides of it. You want her to come over to your side. She wants you to come over to her side. And guess what? Never gonna happen. So what do you do? Compromise. You take one step forward. She takes one step forward. Then you. Then her. Then you... until eventually, you meet at the middle. No one got exactly what they wanted, but at least now you're together again and can go out and have fun!

Famous Compromises Between the Friends 4-Ever*

Have You Met My Pet Peeves?

We love dogs. We love cats. We even love tarantulas and slimy snakes—as long as they stay in their cages. But there are just some pets that we can't stand at all: our pet peeves! A pet peeve is some person's little behavior that drives you crazy. You know, that *one thing* that people do that just makes you want to smash a pillow over your head until they go away.

Our Pet Peeves:

Libby: when someone picks at their nails and just leaves the little pieces of nail lying all over your bedroom (*Uh, not that I'm talking about Rachel or anything.*)

Rachel: people interrupting me

Sam: when someone tries to talk to me during a movie

JESSIE: PEOPLE WHO SLURP THEIR SOUP

A pet peeve can make you supermad, superfast—but the important thing to remember is that the person bugging you probably doesn't even know it! So if you get so annoyed that you can't ignore it, don't start yelling and screaming. Instead, just be polite: "Excuse me, but would you mind not doing that? It's my pet peeve." No yelling, no fighting—and, if you're lucky, no more little pieces of fingernail lying around your bedroom.

Since You Asked ★ ★ ★

Dear Friends 4-Ever,

My BFF is driving me crazy. Whenever we do our homework together, she starts humming to herself. It starts off quiet, but then gets so loud I can't even think! I definitely can't finish my homework. The worst part is, she's totally tone-deaf. I don't even know if she realizes she's doing it, and I don't want to hurt her feelings. But did I mention that it's DRIVING ME CRAZY? I need help, and soon, before I flunk out of school!

Yours truly,

Silence Is Golden

Dear Silence Is Golden,

Your letter is music to our ears! This problem has an easy fix. Just tell your BFF how you feel. Make sure you're really nice about it so you don't hurt her feelings. You could say something like, "This sounds kind of silly, but you know how you hum when you do your homework? It makes it hard for me to focus." In this case, honesty really is the best policy. And if that doesn't work, you have three options: 1) Next time you're doing homework together, turn on the radio. 2) Start doing your homework by yourself. 3) Buy some earplugs!

Good luck,

Samantha   Rachel   Jessie   Libby

Breathe In, Breathe Out

I used to get mad at everything. No, I mean it. Everything. If someone stepped on my toe? Mad. If someone accidentally kicked the back of my chair? Mad. If someone was talking behind me while I was trying to watch a movie? Mad. (Okay, that one still makes me kind of mad.) But life wasn't too much fun when I was getting angry all the time. And it wasn't much fun for my friends, either. After all, I kept yelling at them!

Sometimes when I saw Sam coming, I'd run the other way!

So I learned how to calm myself down. It's called anger management, and it means that instead of yelling and screaming, you stay calm. You think before you speak. And best of all, you get to keep all your friends, because you're not yelling at them all the time. Here's how I did it:

● Breathe in, breathe out. Breathing slowly and deeply for a while can calm your body down, which will make you calm, too.

● Stop using words like "never" and "always." For example, "The pencil sharpener always breaks when I try to use it!" and "You never let me have the last cookie!" are things you should try not to say. You want to think positively.

● Accept that not every problem's going to have an obvious solution. Be patient.

● Remind yourself that the world is not out to get you. And not everything that happens is done on purpose.

● Make yourself laugh. If you're tempted to call someone names, don't. Instead, imagine what it might be like if that name actually came true. For example, instead of saying something mean like, "You're as dumb as a rock!" just stay quiet and picture what it would look like if that person turned into a big rock with little arms and legs and a funny face. Laughing is always better than yelling.

All's Well That Ends Well

You listened to everyone's points of view. You made your compromises. You managed your anger. You said you were sorry. Now it's time for the best part: making up! After every great fight, you and your friends deserve a great way of making up. Here's how we celebrated the end of our biggest fights:

movie marathon

scrapbook of friendship memories

make-your-own-pizza party

friendship time capsule

(This is a box or container you fill with meaningful tokens of your friendship and hide or bury someplace special. In a year, five years, or even ten years, you can dig it up to share your friendship treasures.)

friendship bracelets

makeover night

trip to the beach

Rachel took this picture of us making up!

It's a small world, after all. So why not know how to say "I'm sorry" in more than one language?

Italian:

Spiacente.
[spee-ah-CHEHN-tay]

French:

Je suis désolé.
[ZHUH SWEE day-zo-LAY]

Spanish:

Lo siento.
[LOW see-EHN-toe]

Fair-Fight Resolutions

Use this space to make some promises to yourself and your BFF. What will you and your friends do to make sure that all your fights this year are fair fights?

My fair fight resolutions. This year, my friends and I will . . .

_____

_____

_____

_____

_____

_____

_____

_____

_____

_____

_____

_____

_____

_____

A FRIEND IN NEED

Every friendship has its rainy days. But sometimes the problem isn't that you disagree with each other. Sometimes it's just one of you that's having the problem. And when one of your friends is having a terrible, horrible, no good, very bad day, it means you've got a job to do: **help!**

How can you help? Sometimes by cheering up your friend, sometimes just by being a good listener. The important thing is to let her know that you're there for her, whatever she needs. After all, isn't that what friends are for?

Sometimes when I'm sad, I feel like I'm all alone in the world.

you're never alone—you'll always have us!

In some ways, we're all the same. After all, we all have days when we're just really, really sad. But no one is sad in exactly the same way. And no one likes to be cheered up in exactly the same way.

When I'm sad . . .

I like to shut myself up in my bedroom and read one of my favorite books.

I sneak off to be by myself. But secretly, I always wish that my friends will come find me and listen to me talk about my problems.

I hate being alone. I want all my friends to come over and cheer me up. If we joke around enough, it helps me forget what I was sad about in the first place.

I ride my bike. I pedal as hard as I can and as fast as I can, and I don't stop until I'm too tired to be upset anymore.

How do you act when *you're* upset?

_____

_____

_____

_____

How do you like to be cheered up?

_____

_____

_____

_____

Ask your friends these questions, too.

Then when *they* are sad, you'll know exactly what to do.

HUMANS MAY BE THE ONLY ANIMALS ON EARTH THAT CRY TEARS WHEN WE'RE SAD. AND EVEN SCIENTISTS DON'T REALLY KNOW WHY WE DO IT!

Sometimes people's problems are really, really big. So big that you can't cheer them up—so big that you're scared to try. When Sam's grandmother died, we didn't know what we were supposed to do, or what we were supposed to say. We had never even seen Sam cry before, and suddenly she was crying all the time! Finally, we wrote her this letter:

Dear Sam,
We are really sorry about your grandmother. We know how much you loved her. She was really great. Remember that time she made us cookies? They were so good. We don't know what to say to make you feel better, but we wish we did. Because we love you a lot. You are our best friend, and we will do whatever you need us to do. We will do ANYTHING. We just wanted you to know that you're not alone.

Lots of love and big, big hugs,

Libby   Jessie   Rachel

You guys are the best friends EVER!

Since You Asked ...

Dear Friends 4-Ever,

My BFF's dog just died, and she's really sad. I don't know what I'm supposed to do to cheer her up. I tried to say something nice about Hector (that's her dog), but she just started crying. Was that the wrong thing to do? Do you think she's mad at me now? Should I just stay away from her until she feels better?

Hope you can help,

Fears of Tears

Dear Fears of Tears,

Don't worry, you didn't do anything wrong. It's okay for your BFF to be sad for awhile and remember how much she loved her dog. And maybe she doesn't want to be cheered up yet. You should just tell her the truth—that you love her, and you want to help her, but you don't know how. Ask her if there's anything she needs you to do.

And if there's not, just give her a big hug and remind her that she can say anything to you. Sometimes when people are sad, you don't have to say anything or do anything—sometimes they just need you to listen.

You can do it,

Samantha   Rachel   Jessie   Libby

What Did You Say?

Sometimes the most important thing a friend can do is be a good listener. But that's tougher than it sounds. Talking is easy. Listening—really listening—can be a little trickier. Here are some easy ways you can make yourself a better listener:

DON'T . . .

. . . be judgmental. Don't start telling your friend what she's doing wrong or how you could do it better.

. . . assume you already know what your friend is going to say.

. . . get distracted while your friend is talking because you're thinking about what you want to say next.

. . . feel like you have to come up with a solution to every problem. Sometimes just letting someone talk about a problem can be the best solution of all.

. . . be afraid of silence. It's okay if your friend doesn't feel like talking.

. . . interrupt!

DO . . .

. . . pay attention to the things your friend isn't saying out loud. Body language can tell you a lot.

. . . make eye contact, and make it clear that you're paying attention. (And *do* pay attention.)

. . . ask questions, if it seems like your friend needs help getting all her thoughts and feelings out.

. . . make sure your friend knows you won't tell anyone else about what she said, unless she wants you to.

DID YOU KNOW PEOPLE SPEAK WITH THEIR BODIES? HERE'S HOW YOU CAN "LISTEN" TO BODY LANGUAGE:

- leaning forward = ready to listen
- foot tapping = bored
- arms crossed = lack of trust
- eye contact = paying attention
- hands on hips = stubborn
- rubbing back of neck = frustrated
- touching face = may be lying

Quiz Time: Listen Up!

Are you a good listener? We want to know!

1 **Your best friend calls you and says she has something superimportant to tell you. You . . .**

a) Jump in first to tell her all about what happened to you in the cafeteria that afternoon, then hang up before remembering to ask why she called.

b) Spend half an hour listening to her complain about getting grounded, then spend another half hour complaining about the fight you had with your parents.

c) Let her tell you all about her bad day, and never mention that you need her help with math. She has enough to worry about.

2 **In history class, when the teacher talks, you . . .**

a) Whisper to all of your friends. If the teacher's talking, you're sure he won't even notice.

b) Try to pay attention but get distracted thinking about whether you should go to the mall tomorrow.

c) Do your best to write down every single thing he says, then freak out because he's talking too fast.

3 **You find your friend in the girls' bathroom, crying. She claims that nothing's wrong. You . . .**

a) Shrug your shoulders and go back to checking yourself out in the mirror.

b) Give her a hug and tell her that when she's ready to talk, you're ready to listen.

c) Offer to stay in there with her until she feels better, even though you really should get back to French class, where you're in the middle of a test.

4 **It's your BFF's birthday. You . . .**

a) Throw her a surprise party, even though she told you a million times she didn't want one. After all, who doesn't like a party?

b) Buy her a CD you know she wants, because a few weeks ago she saw it in the store and got all excited.

c) Spend the day with her at an amusement park, like she wanted, and never mention that roller coasters make you want to throw up.

5 **You got into a big fight with your sister, so you ask your BFF for advice. When she gives you some, you . . .**

a) Ignore it, because it sounds like hard work. What does she know, anyway?

b) Think carefully about what she says. Ask lots of other people for advice, too, and then decide what you should do.

c) Do whatever she says. Even if it doesn't sound like the greatest idea, you're sure she knows best.

Mostly *A*s: Extra Earwax

You never hear anything anyone says. Be careful you're
not always putting yourself above your friends. Being a
good friend means being a good listener, so take some
time to close your mouth and open your ears.

Mostly *B*s: Goddess of Listening

Your friends come to you when they have problems,
because they know you'll lend them a sympathetic ear.
But you also know when it's time to ask your friends
to listen to you. Best of all, you don't just hear what
they're saying, you do your best to understand it.

Mostly *C*s: Ms. Invisible

You listen to everyone—except yourself.
You think anything your friends want
to talk about is more important than
anything you might have to say. Try
giving yourself some time for support
from your friends, too. You can't be a
good friend to others without being a
good friend to yourself.

Hmm, mostly As. . . Wait—
I have extra earwax? Uh-oh!

The Amazing Power of Brainpower

PEOPLE LIKE TO SAY, "NOT EVERY PROBLEM HAS A SOLUTION." WHAT DO I SAY? THEY'RE JUST NOT TRYING HARD ENOUGH. WHEN YOU PUT YOUR BRAIN TO WORK, YOU CAN DO ANYTHING. HERE ARE THE KINDS OF THINGS I DO WHEN I PUT ON MY THINKING CAP:

• Write down exactly what's wrong.

• Figure out if it's just one big problem or lots of little ones all together.

• Put the problems in order of importance, then start with the biggest one.

• Brainstorm a list of possible solutions. Write down anything that I think of, even if it sounds silly.

• Go through the list and choose the four best ideas.

• For each of the best solution ideas, make a list of what's good and what's bad about it.

• Ask other people for advice, in case they notice something I don't.

• Decide on a plan.

• List all the steps I need to carry out the plan.

• Figure out what caused the problem in the first place. Ask myself what I can do to keep this from happening again.

THIS DOESN'T WORK EVERY TIME. SOMETIMES WHEN SOMETHING GOES WRONG, I HAVE A LOT OF TROUBLE COMING UP WITH THE RIGHT ANSWER—BUT I NEVER STOP LOOKING!

45

Here's how Jessie helped me solve one of my biggest problems!

LIBBY'S PROBLEM: MUST GET BETTER GRADES IN SOCIAL STUDIES

Possible solutions:
* Ask teacher for help.
* Study more for tests.
* Fake being sick on day of next test.
* Do lots of extra credit.

LIBBY'S PLAN:

1. Read part of the chapter every night, instead of waiting for the night before the test.

2. Make flashcards.

3. No whispering in class instead of listening to the teacher.

4. Ask Jessie to quiz me.

5. Start studying three nights before the test.

6. No TV the night before a big test.

7. If plan doesn't work on next test, ask teacher for extra help.

Quiz Time: Solve This!

WHEN YOU HAVE A PROBLEM, DO YOU ACT WITHOUT THINKING OR THINK WITHOUT ACTING? ANSWER THESE QUESTIONS, AND WE'LL HELP YOU FIGURE IT OUT!

1 It's the day of the big field trip, but you left your permission slip at home, and without it, you won't be able to go on the trip.
You...

a) Start hyperventilating and burst into tears.

b) Sneak out of school and run home to get the permission slip, even though you know you'll probably get into big trouble if anyone catches you.

c) Talk to your teacher and ask whether there's any way to contact your parents and get permission for the trip.

2 Your two best friends can't stand each other. On your birthday, you want to go to dinner with both of them, but they won't go for that. Instead, they claim you just have to go to dinner with the one you like the best. You . . .

a) Decide it's not worth the trouble and spend your birthday sitting home alone.

b) Don't have the nerve to decide, so you lie. You tell each of them that she's your favorite, and go to two dinners in one night.

c) Tell both of them how this is ruining your birthday, and suggest that, just for one night, they have a truce.

3 You have a huge math test tomorrow, and you just opened your book for the first time. Turns out you don't understand anything in the chapter! You . . .

a) Freak out and try to cram it all in, but you're so panicked that you just stare at the pages for hours without getting it.

b) Decide that you'll either fake being sick to get out of the test or try to cheat.

c) Call a friend or a parent and ask them to help

you study. If that doesn't work, you talk to your teacher after the test and request extra help.

4 **Your BFF asks you to sleep over, but you're grounded for the weekend. You really want to go, so you . . .**

a) Tell her that you'll ask your parents. But you're pretty sure they'll say no, so in the end, you don't even bother.

b) Lie to your parents and tell them you have an extra-credit project that you need to work on with your friend—all night long.

c) Tell your parents why it is so important for you to go out this weekend, and try to make a deal. Maybe you can be grounded next weekend?

5 **You accidentally break your friend's mother's favorite vase. When she runs into the room to see what broke, you . . .**

a) Start to cry so hard that you can't even tell her what happened, then run out of the room.

b) Panic, and tell her that the dog did it.

c) Explain what happened, apologize, and offer to find a way to pay for it.

**Now count up the number of
As, Bs, and Cs you answered.**

Mostly As: Trapped in Your Head

When you have a problem, you freak out. You think of all the bad things that could possibly happen if you do the wrong thing, so you do nothing. But that's not going to help you solve your problem. We all make mistakes sometimes—but you have to trust yourself. You have to take a chance. Most of all, you have to act!

Mostly Bs: Basic Instinct

You feel that "think before you speak" is for suckers. When something goes wrong, you don't think, you just do the first thing that pops into your head. And you never think about the consequences. There's just one problem: Taking the easy way out usually just causes more trouble in the long run!

Mostly Cs: Cool Customer

When something goes wrong, you follow one simple rule: Don't panic. You stay cool, calm, and collected. You try to break down the problem, think through your options, and decide how to fix things. You never do anything without thinking very carefully about what might happen if you act. Sometimes you make the wrong choice, but usually it all works out in the end.

The Artist Inside

When I'm really sad, sometimes I don't want to talk to anybody. I just shut myself in my room, and I take out all my art supplies. Then I paint and paint until eventually I feel better. I know it sounds kind of weird, but it actually works.

You don't have to be a good artist to paint your feelings. In fact, you don't even have to paint. There are a lot of ways to be creative. You could:

Make a collage.

Write a poem.

Play a song.

Write a story or write in a journal or diary.

When I paint, I can get out all the things that are too hard to say out loud. When I'm really angry, I use a lot of red and orange. I splash it across the page, like the picture is angry, too. And when I'm sad, I paint with lots of blue and gray watercolors. Sometimes the paint looks like tears. We all have an artist inside—even you!

SCIENTISTS SAY THAT BEING CREATIVE REALLY CAN MAKE YOU FEEL BETTER!

Trust Me!

Friends can't help each other if they don't trust each other. And they can't listen to each other if they don't know how to talk to each other. So here are some ways to build trust, improve communication, and have fun!

Human Maze

1. Blindfold your friend.

2. Without touching her, guide her from one point in the house to another.

You're in charge of telling her which way to walk and which way to turn so that she doesn't bump into anything!

Don't try this on the stairs— trust me!

On the Run

1. Find a wide-open, flat space.

2. Have your friend blindfold you. Now hold hands and start walking. Let your friend guide you.

3. Walk faster and faster, until you're jogging or even running.

   Do you trust your friend to make sure you don't fall?

Secret Sharer

1. Have all your friends write down five questions on five pieces of paper. They can be anything from "What's your favorite movie?" to "What are you afraid of?"

2. Put the papers in a shoe box and mix them up.

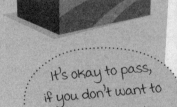

3. Close your eyes and pick one. Then answer that question for the group.

4. When you're done, pass the box to someone else.

It's okay to pass, if you don't want to answer the question.

Measure for Measure

1. Get your group of friends together and put a blindfold on everyone.

2. Without talking or peeking, try to line up in order of height. How quickly can you do it?

Since You Asked . . .

Dear Friends 4-Ever,

I tell my friends everything—all except one of them. I don't tell her anything, because she has a big mouth. Seriously, if I tell her something, I might as well be telling the whole school! So now I keep my most important stuff secret from her, and so do our other friends. I think she feels kind of out of the loop, but I don't know what else to do.

Yours truly,

Blabbermouth's Buddy

Dear Blabbermouth's Buddy,

First things first, you should figure out if your friend is spilling your secrets on purpose. If she is, then it might make sense for you to stop trusting her. But maybe she's doing it by accident. Talk to your friend and let her know how much it upsets you when she gossips about your life. If she has trouble remembering what's secret and what's not, maybe you can figure out some ways to remind her. Before you totally cut her out of the loop, give her a chance to change.

Your secret's safe with us,

Samantha   Rachel   Jessie   Libby

Even best friends can be better friends, if they try. What are five ways you can be a better friend to your BFF? In the second column, have your BFF list five ways she can be a better friend to you. See what happens when you give them a try.

YOU

1._____

2._____

3._____

4._____

5._____

BFF

1._____

2._____

3._____

4._____

5._____

PROBLEM-SOLVING 101

Ever think that life seems a whole lot easier when you're on vacation?

There's nothing like fun in the sun!

You need to go to school, of course—and hopefully, you even like going to school (at least some of the time). But it can definitely be Problem Central. So what's the solution? You could try playing sick every time you have a problem . . .

Cough. Cough. Poor me, I think I have yellow-spotted fever.

I hope Mom doesn't notice these spots are drawn in marker!

. . . but then you'd probably just end up grounded. For life. Trust us, there's a better way. Welcome to Problem-Solving 101, guaranteed to help you figure a way out of a lot of sticky situations.

Are You Too Bossy?

Choose true or false for each of these statements:

1. When you hang out with your friends, you almost always pick the activity.
   TRUE **FALSE**

2. You don't want to be friends with anyone who disagrees with you too much.
   TRUE **FALSE**

3. You think the coolest people are the ones who are a lot like you.
   TRUE **FALSE**

4. If you invite your friend to do something, and she doesn't want to, you don't give up until she changes her mind.
   TRUE **FALSE**

5. People are scared to say no to you.
   TRUE **FALSE**

6. You have a habit of telling your friends that they "should" do this or that.
   TRUE   FALSE

7. When you don't get your way, you always pout.
   TRUE   FALSE

8. You get easily frustrated, angry, or annoyed with your friends.
   TRUE   FALSE

9. In your group of friends, you like it best when you're doing most of the talking or decision-making.
   TRUE   FALSE

10. In a conversation, sometimes your friends have to tell you to stop interrupting them.
    TRUE   FALSE

If you answered "true" to any of these, then watch out: You may be bossy! Try to remember that your friends have ideas and opinions just like you do. Sometimes they won't always want to do the same things as you. It doesn't make them bad friends. But it does make *you* a bad friend if you try to force them to do something they don't want to do!

Since You Asked . . .

Dear Friends 4-Ever,

I was so excited when the coolest girl in school invited me to go to the mall with her and her friends. And it was fun, I guess, until we were in the drugstore, and the other girls started sneaking lip gloss and nail polish into their pockets. They tried to get me to take some, too, but I knew it was wrong. I was afraid to say no, so instead I just told them I had to go home. What am I supposed to do if they invite me to the mall again? I don't want to look like I'm not cool. But I don't want to be a thief! Can you help?

Yours Truly,
Honestly Confused

Dear Honestly Confused,

Congratulations, you did the right thing! You should never do something you think is wrong just because you want to look cool. The easiest way to make sure this doesn't happen again is to stop hanging out with those girls. But if you really do want to be friends with them, you shouldn't be afraid to tell them no. And if that doesn't work, then you should make up an excuse and walk away, just like you did before. If they really are friend material, they won't hold it against you. Some things are more important than looking cool—but it sounds like you know that already!

Keep up the good work,
Samantha   Rachel   Jessie   Libby

You have to stand up for what you believe in, no matter what anyone says. Any real friend will understand that no means no!

Bully Blues

Last year, there was this girl who wouldn't stop picking on me. Every day, she would tell me that my shirt was ugly or my shoes were tacky. She would spread nasty rumors about me, and once she even poured a carton of chocolate milk in my lap. She said it was an accident, but I knew the truth.

Sam told me I should just stand up to her and tell her to go away. But that's easy for Sam to say—she's brave. I'm not like that.

Libby told me I should just be nice to her and turn her into my friend. But that's easy for Libby to say—making new friends is a piece of cake for her. I'm not like that, either.

Jessie's the one who told me that I had a bully. I always thought a bully was just someone who beat up little kids for their lunch money. But Jessie said that a bully is anyone who picks on someone else because they seem weak. Jessie also said that it's really the bully who's weak, and that's why they tease everyone else. Once I knew what I was dealing with, my friends and I came up with some ideas for how we could stop my bully:

- Act brave and know you're a strong person. Bullies like to pick on people they think are weak and easy targets.

- Don't let the bully see that she is bothering you. Just ignore her. Eventually, she might get bored and go away.

- Don't fight back, even if you want to. That will just make things worse.

- Use the buddy system. The bully will probably leave you alone if you're surrounded by friends.

- If your bully is spreading rumors about you, try to ignore them. But have your friends tell everyone they're not true.

HAVING A BULLY CAN BE SCARY, AND YOU DON'T HAVE TO DEAL WITH IT YOURSELF. IF YOU DON'T KNOW WHAT TO DO, ALWAYS TELL A PARENT OR A TEACHER WHAT'S GOING ON— THEY REALLY CAN HELP.

Heard It Through the Grapevine

What's more fun than sitting around with some big scoops of ice cream and some even bigger scoops of gossip? It can be fun to talk about other people, especially when you know something that no one else does. But not all gossip is created equal.

It's okay to read magazines and obsess about which movie stars are dating and which are hating. But there's a difference between Hollywood stars and the kids down the hall. Would you really want people talking about all the tiny and embarrassing details of your life? Especially if they weren't even true? Gossip and rumors can get out of control, fast—and they can really hurt people's feelings.

"No way!"

"Did you hear?"   *"I don't believe it!"*   *"You mean she really . . . ?"*

I admit it, I had a big mouth. And I loved it, because everyone came to me for all the hot gossip. But then things got out of control, and I accidentally hurt someone's feelings. So I decided to stop gossiping. It was really, really hard, but I did it. Now when I get the urge to talk about someone, I come up with something nice to say and spread that around instead. A compliment travels way better than gossip, anyday.

ALL ABOUT YOU

What's the biggest fight you've ever had with
your friends? How did you solve it?

I'll never forget the time we _Started_
a rock band.

But we finally made up when _____

What are some ways that you've helped out one
of your friends in need?

1. _playing whith her._
2. _____
3. _____
4. _____
5. _____

What's your problem-solving strategy? Describe
a big problem and how you fixed it:

_____
_____

Wow, your friends are lucky to
have someone like you around!

This book may be all about problems and fights, but just remember: your friendships aren't. Friendships are also about all the good stuff in between the arguments. All the secrets and slumber parties, gossip and giggling, phone calls and fun—everything that makes you and your friends want to be Friends 4-Ever. Forever is a long time, and that's exactly how long you want to keep your friends around—for better and worse, in good times and bad.

That's why it's so important to take care of one another, to fight fair, compromise, listen, and help. So even when you get so mad you think your head is going to explode, or so blue that all you want to do is crawl under the covers and cry, just remember, you need your friends and your friends need you. Because having a true friend means you're never alone, and if you and your friends stick together, you can do anything!

us... together 4-ever!